THE SECURITY CONCERNS OF THE
BALTIC STATES AS NATO ALLIES

The last decade has not seen the end of serious security concerns in northeastern Europe. When the three Baltic States of Latvia, Estonia, and Lithuania joined the North Atlantic Treaty Organization (NATO) and the European Union (EU) in 2004, they brought an increased level of security in the region. But underlying the general state of peace in the region are serious concerns that could undermine European security and the state of the NATO alliance in northeastern Europe.

Security concerns in the Baltic Region are multifaceted. Despite the largely friendly and conciliatory attitude of NATO toward Russia, the Russian regime has taken on a decidedly and openly anti-NATO attitude in the last several years. The recently published military doctrine of the Russian Federation (2010) openly calls NATO an "enemy."[1] There is still considerable friction between the Western Allied NATO states of the Baltic and the Russian Federation and its allies. For example, there are unresolved border issues on the Estonian/Russian border stemming from Russia's unilateral changing of the 1920 Treaty Line. The recent major national cyber attack on Estonia, apparently mounted from Russia, is another point of friction. In the Baltic States, there are large Russian minorities subject to influence and anti-Western propaganda spread by the Russian Federation. Energy security for the region is a constant concern. In addition to the above-named concerns, the three Baltic States also face the same terrorism threat as the rest of the NATO nations. The three Baltic States are also involved in ongoing combat operations in Afghanistan and peacekeeping operation in the Balkans as part of the Western alliance.

SCOPE OF THE MONOGRAPH

It is the intent of the author to provide an assessment of the key security concerns of the three Baltic States in terms of their NATO membership and close ties to the Western alliance. Taking security in its broadest sense—to include economic and diplomatic issues—the key questions are: How do each of the three Baltic States see their primary threats and security concerns? What do these states see as the most serious problem, and what is their justification for this thinking? Where are the security concepts and strategies of the United States and three Baltic States in agreement? Where do they diverge? Is there a particular "Baltic Perspective" within NATO? If so, how does this affect the alliance relations of the three Baltic States with their larger partners?

Methodology.

My methodology was to provide the context of Baltic national views on security by reviewing the concerns on Baltic security of the three Baltic governments through the lens of articles, books, and public documents written by Baltic academics and policymakers and shapers. In addition, I interviewed 15 policymakers and shapers—five from each Baltic nation—in order to develop an assessment, in their words, of how the Baltic governments view the threats to their national security and how they see future developments. The intent of this analysis is to help U.S. makers and shapers of security policy understand the views and concerns of American allies in this region.

INTRODUCTION

In 2004, the three Baltic States of Latvia, Lithuania, and Estonia joined both NATO and the EU as full members. This alignment of the three states with the West was the culmination of three national policies to integrate fully their economies, societies, and national security systems as partners with the West.

Since regaining their national independence in 1991, the three Baltic States have followed a path similar to that of Eastern European nations, which had been subject states of the Warsaw Pact and under de facto Soviet domination after World War II, in becoming fully allied with the West. Not only have all the former Warsaw Pact nations of Eastern Europe joined NATO, but all joined the EU between 2004 and 2007. However, the three Baltic States stand out because these three NATO nations were republics of the Soviet Union until 1991; unlike the other "new" NATO and EU nations, these nations had no legal national existence or national institutions before 1991. These three countries started literally from scratch in 1991 as impoverished former Soviet lands, and have managed a complete transformation in terms of politics, economics, social relations, and foreign and security relations in just over 20 years. In a determined effort that often required painful economic reforms, the three nations have successfully built modern market economies and fully mature democracies.

In some ways, beginning with the reinvention of the Baltic economies, the three Baltic States have aligned more with America than with Western Europe. The model of democratic development that the Baltic States followed since the 1990s was the economic model of the United States and Britain at the time of the economic reforms of President Ronald Reagan and Prime Minister Margaret Thatcher rather than the Western European model. In the 1990s, the more flexible and market oriented Anglo-Saxon model, with lower taxes and a more positive position toward business and investment, was a template for economic growth in contrast to the high-tax and highly regulated social welfare states of Western Europe, which, by the 1990s, had achieved a state of low growth, high unemployment, and economic stagnation in Germany, Italy, and France.[2] While many of the social mores and attitudes of the three Baltic States are more aligned with Western Europe, the economic model is more like America of the 1990s.

In another respect, that of security policy, one can also say the Baltic States are closer to America than to Western Europe. President George Bush, in the early-1990s, supported Baltic independence, even as Western Europeans were reluctant to confront the Soviet Union. It was with the support of President George W. Bush that the three Baltic States joined NATO in 2004. Thus, the policymakers and shapers of the three Baltic States remember that, in terms of their independence and security, the United States was always more supportive than "Old Europe."

The security link to the West, and especially with America, is not forgotten in the Baltic States. Since the 1990s, in all matters of security and foreign policy, the three Baltic nations have stood out as strong and reliable allies of the West, and of the United States in particular. Beginning in the 1990s, the three Baltic States began contributing military forces to NATO and United Nations (UN) peace operations.[3] In 2003, even before joining NATO, the three Baltic States all strongly supported the U.S.-led coalition in Iraq, and all three Baltic States contributed forces to serve under U.S. and coalition command in the Iraq War. All three Baltic nations have been very active in Afghanistan, and all have contributed contingents of hundreds of fighting troops, as well as civilian trainers, to serve under U.S. and NATO command. Unlike so many other European contributors, the three Baltic States come prepared for combat and have no caveats restricting their employment.

Although small nations, (Lithuania, population 3.5 million; Latvia, 2.2 million; and Estonia, 1.4 million), the three countries make a serious effort to support the Western security system, by striving, at least before the onset of the economic crisis, to meet the goal of 2 percent of gross domestic product (GDP) for defense.[4] The three Baltic nations consistently support U.S. security strategy and international efforts and can be counted on to support U.S. security efforts not only in Europe, but also in Africa and Central Asia. As of this writing, there are hundreds of Baltic troops in Afghanistan, and there are Baltic naval teams supporting the international anti-piracy campaign in the Gulf of Aden. In dealing with consistent allies, it is important for the United States and NATO nations to understand the viewpoints and specific concerns of the three Baltic States. They may be small, but they still count.

This monograph aims to provide an overview of the concerns and perceptions of the people in the three Baltic States who serve as the policymakers and policy shapers in terms of national and international security. I interviewed 15 people from the Baltic States, each of whom is involved in making or shaping security policy for their nation. I chose five people from each nation to interview, selecting senior government officials, senior military officers, and academics who serve as advisors to their respective governments on security and foreign affairs issues. I interviewed them on a nonattribution basis to obtain as candid a view as possible of their country and the region's security concerns.[5] Official government statements and policy papers of the Baltic States do, indeed, specify many of the threats to and concerns about security, but there is also a tendency to avoid commenting candidly about ongoing security concerns in a desire not to provoke unnecessary tensions with allied or opponent nations. Although several of the interviewees stated that I could use their name and cite them in full if I wished, I chose the nonattribution method as the best means of obtaining the most honest views without generating professional friction for any of the officials and academics.

I lived and worked for 4 years in the Baltic States as the Dean of the Baltic Defence College in Tartu, Estonia. The Baltic Defence College is the institution of higher military learning for the three Baltic States. It is a unique institution, as it is owned and operated jointly by the three Baltic countries. As dean, I worked closely with Baltic States senior officers, Baltic senior officials, and academics from the three Baltic States. Over 4 years, I built up a large network of contacts within the Baltic armed forces, defense ministries, and universities.

In addition, I also teach graduate courses as an adjunct faculty member of Tartu University, one of the oldest and most important centers of higher learning in Eastern Europe. Through my position, I have special access to key people in the Baltic States who make and shape security policy. Most of the people I interviewed I have known for years, and every one I asked was quite willing to participate in this project. The policymakers I refer to are senior officers from the three Baltic States, senior government officials, and a member of a national parliament. All have been directly involved in developing the national security policies of their own countries. The policy shapers I have talked to are academics who are involved in scholarship concerning national security issues, and most have served on commissions and boards to advise their national governments on security policy.

All those I interviewed have impressive academic backgrounds, are well published, and are highly respected in their profession. All have broad European and international experience. All are multilingual, speaking fluent English and most also fluent Russian, as well as their national language. All were able to converse fluently in English for the interviews. All of the Baltic military senior officers are representative of the higher ranks of the Baltic States' armed forces who have graduated from Western European or U.S. staff and war colleges. All the military personnel have served overseas, normally a tour at NATO headquarters in Belgium and tours of duty in Iraq or Afghanistan, or both. All the military people and the senior government officials have spent considerable time working closely with the U.S. Armed Forces and know America well. All the Baltic academics have spent considerable time in U.S. and Western European universities, either as students or on faculty exchange programs. In short, these are people with exceptionally broad international experience who can be matched with the best qualified U.S. and Western European experts. For these reasons, their views are important and worth considering.

Indeed, in one way, the Baltic academics and policymakers have an advantage over their Western European policymakers and shapers. As one Latvian senior official put it:

> The Baltics have a special perspective because we really know the Russians. Unlike the Poles and Hungarians, who were Warsaw Pact nations that had at least nominal independence and their own national institutions, until recently we were part of the Soviet Union. We were inside the system. We were brought up having to learn fluent Russian. The Communist Party of the USSR [Union of Soviet Socialist Republics] dominated our countries. After that long experience, we know how the Russians think, and we can read between the lines. Even the other Eastern Europeans cannot get inside the minds of the Russians like we can.[6]

HISTORICAL CONTEXT OF BALTIC SECURITY

Between Russia and Western Europe, an Unhappy History.

It is important to understand that the Baltic States are culturally Western, not Eastern. Latvia and Estonia were brought into the broader European culture and economy by the Germans and Danes in the 12th and 13th centuries. Until the 1700s, Latvia and Estonia were first under German and then later Swedish domination. Then, with the conquest of Latvia and Estonia by Peter the Great in the early-18th century, that region became part of the Russian Empire. Lithuania had become Christian and been united with Poland in the 14th century. With the destruction of the Polish state in the late-18th century, Lithuania also came under the Russian Empire. However, even as part of the Russian Empire, the three Baltic States retained their culture and religion (Latvia and Estonia were Lutheran; Lithuania was Catholic). Because of religion, culture, and traditional trade relationships, the Baltic States were always oriented toward the West, not the East.

Latvia and Estonia, along with Finland, became the most modern, literate, and advanced regions of the Old Russian Empire. A cultural revival in the 19th century awakened a sense of nationalism in all three countries. All retained their languages and national culture as very separate from the Russian culture and developed their own distinctive national literature in the 19th century. The Latvian, Lithuanian, and Estonian languages (none of which are Slavic) all use Latin letters, not Cyrillic. All the countries became independent of Russia in the aftermath of World War I, all fought against the Soviet Union, and in 1919-20 defeated Soviet attempts to invade and restore those republics to Russia.[7]

There followed a 20-year period of independence in which the three Baltic nations developed as Western countries with some measure of prosperity, in contrast to the violence, collectivization, and poverty prevalent in Russia under Joseph Stalin. In 1939, the fate of the Baltic States was sealed by the [Vyacheslav] Molotov - [Joachim von] Ribbentrop Pact of August 1939, which divided Europe into spheres of influence to be controlled by Stalin and Adolf Hitler. The three Baltic States were part of Europe designated as the Soviet sphere of influence, along with Eastern Poland and parts of Romania and Finland. The Soviet Union was given the green light by Hitler to annex those regions. Stalin immediately invaded Finland in November 1939 and, after a brief and bloody war, succeeded in annexing key parts of Finnish territory as part of the

Soviet Union. At the same time, Stalin pressured the Baltic States into allowing large Soviet military bases in their countries. By June 1940, the neutral and militarily weak Baltic States were invaded and occupied by Stalin's forces. The Baltic governments were dissolved, and the national leaders arrested and murdered. After phony elections, the three nations were annexed and became republics of the Soviet Union.[8] This destruction of three independent countries was never recognized as valid by the Western nations.

Under Soviet domination, the three Baltic States suffered horrendous oppression as the national elites were either murdered or sent to gulags. Collectivization and nationalization of farms and industries and businesses were imposed. Large sectors of the population, to include priests and ministers, businessmen, many professionals, intellectuals, military officers, and landowners, were marked for mass arrest and deportation.[9] The only respite came from the German invasion of the Soviet Union in June 1941, which quickly overran the Baltic States and placed the countries under German control until 1944. After the Soviets re-established power in the three Baltic States, a new wave of repression occurred, lasting until the death of Stalin in 1953.[10] This period was characterized by mass arrests and the deportation of hundreds of thousands of Lithuanians, Latvians, and Estonians, either to the gulags or Siberia.[11] The Baltic peoples strongly resisted the Soviet occupation, and large nationalist resistance movements formed in all three Baltic States. For almost a decade after the end of World War II, the Soviets faced armed anti-communist guerrilla forces, called the "Forest Brothers," in the forest lands and rural areas of the Baltic States. Not until 1953, after major efforts by the KGB and military, were the Forest Brothers effectively suppressed.

The rest of the Soviet era was one of forced communization and repression. Because the three Baltic States were far more economically advanced than Russia, the three countries became a center for Soviet high-tech and military industries. Thousands of Russian workers were brought into Latvia and Estonia to work in the military complexes. The northeastern corner of Estonia around Narva and Sillimae (the Soviet Union's first uranium mine and processing plant) was cleared of Estonians, who were replaced by Russians. Large numbers of Russians were also settled to work in industries in Latvia. Only Lithuania escaped the large-scale influx of Russian workers, largely because the Forest Brothers caused so much trouble in the countryside that Stalin's plans to settle large numbers of Russians on collectivized land were foiled.[12]

Still, although the Soviet regime made major efforts to Russify the Baltic States through the post-Stalin period to the 1980s, the people of the Baltic States kept their languages and cultures alive and, underneath the Soviet façade, maintained a strong sense of nationalism and national identity. In the late-1980s, when Premier Mikhail Gorbachev announced reforms in the USSR, the Baltic peoples responded by organizing noncommunist political parties (quite illegal even under Gorbachev) and initiating mass demonstrations opposing Soviet rule. Lithuania declared its independence in 1990 and held free elections. However, KGB troops tried to suppress the new government in Vilnius in January 1991. Bloody repression attempts met with overwhelming national mobilization against the Soviet government in all three Baltic States. Militia units formed spontaneously and deployed themselves to protect the newly elected national parliaments, town councils, and other new democratic institutions.

All three Baltic States set up independent noncommunist national governments. With the failed attempt by hard-line Communists to take back control of the Soviet government in the coup of August 1991, the three Baltic States broke completely with Moscow and were quickly recognized as independent nations by the Nordic, then Western, nations. The reform government in Moscow under Boris Yeltsin quickly recognized the Baltic States as independent nations and withdrew all the Russian armed forces from the Baltic nations in 1994.

With independence came new opportunities to recreate a relationship with Russia, the USSR's successor state. One of the key factors is the burden of history. From recent history, the Baltic peoples have every reason to fear and mistrust Russia. On the other hand, they live next to Russia and have important economic and social relationships with Russia. To get beyond the deep divide of modern history required an acknowledgement not only of Baltic national independence, but also of the enormous crimes committed by Russia against the Baltic States from 1940 to 1991. A first step was taken in building a new foundation under President Gorbachev in 1989, when a Russian government commission, for the first time, acknowledged the secret protocols of the 1939 Molotov-Ribbentrop Pact that had allowed Stalin to seize the Baltic States. Indeed, the People's Congress of the USSR, in December 1989 under Gorbachev's leadership, denounced the secret Soviet/Nazi protocols as unjustified and invalid.[13] The moves under Gorbachev and later under Boris Yeltsin did much to lower tensions and to begin the establishment of friendly relations in the Baltic area.

These positive developments in Russian/Western relations ended in 2000 with the rise of Vladimir Putin as leader of the Russian state. Liberalization measures and tentative steps toward open government and democracy were systematically quashed. One of Putin's main concerns has been supporting a new Russian nationalist version of history, which was essentially the old Soviet line. Under the current Russian regime, history has again been relegated to the role of serving the state. The tone and substance of Russian state history publications since 2000 — and almost all scholarship is under the control of the state and state-allied agencies — is one of aggressive nationalism. In the interpretation of history promoted by the Russian government under Putin's leadership, the official view is that the Soviet occupation of the Baltic States was fully justified, and those Baltic claims of Soviet crimes against humanity (which are carefully documented and detailed by national commissions in the Baltic States) are exaggerated. Indeed, the Russian historical approach under Putin is to portray all the Baltic peoples as Nazi supporters in World War II, and any critique of the Soviet Union and its role in the Baltics is a "revival of fascism."[14] Baltic attempts to publish accurate histories and to gain international recognition of the crimes committed against the Baltic peoples have been met by a Russian information war to discredit the Baltic States internationally. In 2009, Russian Prime Minister Dmitri Medvedev even set up a historical commission to combat the supposed "falsification of history" that shows the Soviet regime in a bad light.[15] This is in accord with the new Russian history of the Putin era that now portrays Stalin in a positive light as a great national leader and commander in World War II.

Needless to say, this portrayal does not go down well in countries where the memories of Soviet repression and brutality are still very fresh.[16] While honest scholarship briefly flourished in Russia in the 1990s, since the rise of Putin, Russian historical study has been replaced with a state controlled version of events that matches the old Soviet world view in its crudity and readiness to vilify any dissent. The crude propaganda of the Russian official history is likely to appeal to the Russian population, serving to whip up dislike and fear of the West among Russians and to portray the Baltic peoples as fascist servants of the West. It does nothing to enhance the standing of Russia as a reasonable and responsible nation. Nor is Putin's approach helpful in building trust in the region.[17]

The hope in the early-1990s that one could forge a future with a reformed and responsible Russia has been pretty well quashed. The Russian regime is disliked and distrusted in the Baltic States; yet, the Baltic States also acknowledge that they have to walk a fine line to maintain good economic relations with Russia and to keep tensions down. That is why one rarely finds provocative statements by Baltic government leaders and officials about Russia in the news, although academics and political leaders are generally more frank about their views on the nature of the Russian regime.

The Baltic Transition to the West.

The initial foreign policy of the three Baltic States was a state of neutrality, coupled with the goal of creating fully modern democratic states and economic and political integration with the West.[18] This was moved forward with the withdrawal of the last Russian military garrisons in 1994. The next year, the Baltic States made their first applications to join NATO, formally joined the Partnership for Peace program, and set a goal to reform the security system and government to meet NATO standards. The Baltic desire to join NATO, and the likelihood of such an event, was met with general skepticism in Western Europe and the United States.

The Russian government in 1997 offered security guarantees to ensure the Baltic States' independence and security, with the main intent to keep the Baltic States neutral and out of NATO and with the likely unspoken intent to also keep them inside the Russian sphere of influence. The Russian proposal was immediately rejected by the three Baltic States, which led to some unpleasant economic and diplomatic friction between Russia and the Baltics.[19] The Russians persisted in their efforts to keep the Baltic States neutral, but without success. In fact, the Russian proposals, which had been met so coldly by the Baltic governments, served to redouble the Baltic goal to join NATO as full members. From the mid-1990s, the three Baltic States made a concerted effort to create economic and security policies and institutions that met the NATO and EU standards.[20] Remarkably, on May 1, 2004, all three Baltic States were able to join NATO, along with a group of former Warsaw Pact states: Poland, the Czech Republic, Slovakia, and Hungary. Bulgaria and Romania joined in 2007.

Since their independence in the 1990s, there has been fairly close cooperation between the three Baltic States, especially in terms of security issues. The presidents of the states meet regularly and, even before joining NATO, the chiefs of staff and defense ministers of the three Baltic States have met on a quarterly basis to discuss common military and broader security concerns. In the 1990s, the three Baltic States created a joint battalion to support international peacekeeping operations.[21] The development of a joint air defense was begun even before membership in NATO. The three Baltic States have conducted joint exercises and training, cooperated as a Baltic naval force, and, in 1999, the three states created a single staff college and higher defense education institution, the Baltic Defence College located in Tartu, Estonia. It is equally owned and operated by the three Baltic defense ministries, which share equally in the college's management and budget. It is the only multinational military institution of its type.[22] Although many Baltic officers would like to see even more Baltic national cooperation of defense matters, the current cooperation is fairly extensive.[23] In real terms, through this regional identification, close cooperation, and common history, the three Baltic States did form something of a block within NATO and the EU.

In national political cultures, all the Baltic States have center-right governments, strong free market orientation, and strong connections to NATO and the EU. One Estonian academic put it this way:

> the Baltic States were all neutral and isolated in the interwar period in the first era of independence. The Baltic peoples all know[24] what their period of neutrality got them—the loss of freedom and 5 decades of Soviet occupation. This is deep in the national con-

sciousness of the three nations and the view is 'never again'. So the Baltic States all seek to ally themselves with the West and are eager to participate in every kind of international partnership that will strengthen their connections to the West.

THE BALTICS AND RUSSIA

New NATO Strategic Concept 2010.

In the run-up to the crafting of a new strategic concept by NATO, the three Baltic States, along with the Eastern European NATO members, mounted a quiet but effective lobbying effort to influence the new NATO strategic concept to ensure that it would recognize the ongoing strategic threat of Russia and that NATO would maintain its focus on conventional military deterrence.[25] Ironically, this effort was aided by the 2008 Russian invasion of Georgia, an action that shocked the Baltics and caused a brief rupture in NATO/U.S. and Russian relations.

This was the first state-on-state war in Europe in almost a decade—the last conflicts being those of the former Yugoslavian states. This was especially remarkable in that this was the first time a large European nation used the military option and openly invaded and helped cut off two areas recognized as Georgia under international treaties (Abkhazia and South Ossetia). Russia's heavy-handed approach toward NATO and the West helped the Baltic States and the Eastern Europeans to lobby successfully the "Old Europe" NATO nations and the United States to accept collective defense—seen by all the Baltics as being a defense against Russia—as the core mission of the NATO alliance. On the other hand, while NATO does not identify Russia as a threat or enemy and speaks about cooperation with Russia, the last three Russian military doctrines promulgated since 2003—the last approved in 2010—all explicitly state that NATO is Russia's enemy and sees the expansion of NATO into the Baltic States as one of the main threats to Russia.[26]

Context of Baltic Security: A Common View on Security.

The Baltic States, as NATO and EU members, fully accept the security policies of those alliances. However, the national security problems and priorities tend to be different from other NATO and Western European nations. If there is one common Baltic view on the security threat, it is a consensus that Russia is an ongoing threat and problem. Most of the security concerns of the three Baltic States involve Russia in one way or another. It was the consensus of all those interviewed that Russia is a threat to Baltic Region security for the foreseeable future. However, it was also the unanimous view that overt military action by Russia against the Baltic States now and in the future is unlikely in the extreme. The common view is that Russia would prefer to use its soft power, its economic power, its position as a major energy supplier to the region, its information campaigns, and its diplomatic power to undermine the Baltic States and pull the Baltics back into the sphere of Russian influence. In short, in the view of the Baltic policymakers, Russia does not want another occupation of the Baltic States, but rather a situation such as exists in the Ukraine, where Russia can dictate economic and energy policy and has the power to largely control foreign and security policy.

None of those interviewed saw this scenario as likely to happen in the future, but that is clearly the intent of the Russian regime.

The Georgian Invasion and the Baltic States.

Most of the Baltic policymakers and shapers interviewed referred to the conflict in Georgia in 2008 as confirming their view of a less-than-benign Russia. In the summer of 2008, when Russia mounted a full-scale military invasion of Georgia provoked by tensions in the two provinces of Georgia that wanted to break away (Abkhazia and South Ossetia), it sent a shock through Europe and NATO and, for a time, upended NATO/Russia relations, which had been progressing in a somewhat positive manner. Russia came out on top by applying overwhelming military force against a small and weak nation and now occupies the two provinces, where Russia has set up puppet regimes.

However, in some ways, the Georgia invasion has worked against the Russian grand strategy to increase its sphere of influence.[27] Before the Georgia War, the Baltic States were often viewed as being too anti-Russian and alarmist by the NATO allies of "Old Europe." As one Latvian senior officer noted, the Latvians had been warning NATO for months before the invasion about Russian intentions and plans to move on Georgia, and some of the NATO allies (notably some of the "Old Europe" nations of Western Europe) refused to take the threat seriously. Indeed, several of the Baltic policymakers and shapers noted that, in the eyes of many Western Europeans, the Baltics suffered from a credibility problem on the Russia issue due to the nature of their painful relationship with Russia in the past and the suspicion of "Old Europeans" that the

Baltic view is too colored by emotion to be taken seriously. After the Georgia invasion, the Baltics were in the position of being able to say, "We told you so." Georgia was a wakeup call for the Europeans to understand that Russians, and Putin and his circle in particular, were ready to use open and blatant military force to establish their vision of a renewed Russian "sphere of influence" (a common phrase in Russian policy documents) in areas that they had ruled during Russian imperial and Soviet times. Whatever trust that Russia might be an honest and cooperative partner was, at least for a time, shattered. NATO-Russian talks were put on hold for a year. When they were restarted at the behest of the Barack Obama administration, there was still a notable lack of trust concerning Russia and its intentions on the part of the Europeans.

The Georgia conflict and its fallout is another case in which Russian heavy-handedness again worked against the long-term interests of Russia in its dealings with the Baltic States and with the NATO nations. The Russian action in Georgia came just at the moment that NATO was developing its new strategic concept. The Russian invasion of Georgia bolstered the case for the Eastern European NATO members, who could point out the obvious, that the conventional military threat to European security had not gone away. While the NATO new strategic concept was being developed and debated through 2009 and 2010, the Russian action supported the view that conventional military deterrence and response under Article 5 of the Washington Treaty (NATO's founding document) was still relevant and key to NATO's core policy. Thanks to the Russian invasion of Georgia, the new NATO strategic concept published in 2010 included a strong reaffirmation of Article 5 on collective security and deterrence as a core policy of NATO. While the new NATO strategic vision included various global concerns and security concerns out of area, it was actually an evolutionary document and not a dramatically new vision.[28] Without the Russian invasion of Georgia, it is unlikely that the Eastern European view would have prevailed and the core role of Article 5 reaffirmed so strongly.

BALTIC VIEWS ON THEIR NATIONAL SECURITY THREATS

Energy Security.

Energy supply is a key issue that is mentioned by almost all the Baltic leaders and academics as a major national security concern. All the Baltic States depend upon outside sources for their national energy supplies. Lithuania depends fully upon Russia for oil and gas supplies, and Lithuania also purchases a great part of its electricity from Belarus and the Ukraine, Russia's allies. Thus, Lithuania is the state most vulnerable to coercion by means of threatening its energy supplies. Latvia is also highly vulnerable and depends on Russia for the greater part of its gas and oil.[29] Estonia is the least vulnerable in terms of energy, having some of its own supplies of shale oil. Estonia also imports oil and gas through its ports and is less vulnerable than Lithuania and Latvia, which receive oil and gas via pipelines. All the Baltic States are fully aware that the most vulnerable sector of their economy is that of energy supply.[30]

Information Campaign.

Most of those officials interviewed noted the Russian information campaign mounted against the Baltic States as one of the serious threats to their national security. The Baltics have long had to deal with a Russian campaign via news media and television meant to put the Baltic governments in the worst light. Russia generously subsidizes Russian ethnic groups and political parties in the three Baltic States, and Russian television, which puts forward the propaganda picture of the Russian regime, is prominent in all three Baltic States — where it is seen by the Russian minorities. Indeed, Russia has conducted a media campaign against Georgia, Moldova, and Lithuania at times when Russia wanted to coerce those countries to accept Russian policies.[31] The non-Russians are fully aware of the content, as people over 40 speak fluent Russian.[32]

In fact, the ongoing information campaign, complete with false histories, most likely works against Russian long-term interests. The blatant falsification of history reminds people that Russia and the Putin regime are truly the successor state of the Soviet Union, complete with the control of government in the hands of former KGB bureaucrats. The information campaign is unconvincing to anyone outside of the most nationalistic ethnic Russian circles and creates unnecessary friction and distrust between the Baltic nations and Russia. The information campaign, appealing to a false history, does little to bolster Russia's argument that it deserves a "sphere of influence" as the main power of the region. One can understand that many in the Baltics, especially in the governments, tend to see Putin's information campaign in a very emotional light. There is little evidence that anyone in the West takes the Soviet history seriously, or accepts the premise that the Soviet invasion and occupation of the Baltic States was readily accepted by the Baltic peoples. There is also little evidence that anyone in the West believes that Stalin's ruthless program of suppression and mass deportations was justified on any reasonable grounds or real considerations of Soviet defense needs. These were brutal, and even genocidal, acts that are still alive in the memories of the Baltic peoples. Indeed, pushing an information campaign that denies the crimes of the Soviet era works directly against Russian aims to increase its soft power in the region by lowering the credibility of Russia as an honest partner.

One Lithuanian academic and the two Lithuanian senior military officers interviewed noted that the ongoing information campaign mounted by Russia against the Lithuanian government and nation was a serious issue. Several other Baltic policymakers and policy shapers also saw the Russian information campaign against the Baltic States as a problem and threat. The strong anti-Lithuanian information campaign mounted against Lithuania is partly motivated by the friction over the Russian enclave of the Kaliningrad Oblast (formerly Königsberg, Germany), which borders Lithuania. Negotiations over transit and trade to Kaliningrad through Lithuania have been one of the major points of Russian/Baltic States friction since the 1990s. Various agreements have been negotiated, but the Russian approach to negotiations has also been backed up by an information campaign to discredit Lithuania.

The state-supported Russian media print books pushing the view that the occupation of Lithuania under Stalin was a voluntary act endorsed by the

Lithuanians, and that the occupation of Lithuania in 1940 and after World War II was legal and proper. Such blatant lies and falsifications about horrendous crimes against humanity are clearly irritating to the Lithuanian and Baltic peoples. Essentially, the actions by Russia are part of a long-term information campaign to delegitimize the Baltic States in the eyes of the world and with the Russian population. This bolsters Russia's intent to see the Baltics revert to a status of being within the Russian sphere of influence, as well as Russia's policy to style itself as the protector of ethnic Russians outside Russia.

Without the Russian information campaign in the Baltics, the three Baltic governments would not be so worried about Russian investment in the region, and Russian companies buying interests in Baltic companies would not be immediately seen as a compromise of their national security. Apparently, Russians cannot learn that soft power is best employed and wins the greatest results when it is presented as an attractive proposition to the local populations and governments. Soft power backed up by lies, bullying, and coercion is not soft power at all.

Ethnic Minorities and Internal Security.

Latvia and Estonia have significant Russian ethnic minorities that are not well assimilated into the national population and are seen as a security threat, albeit a declining one.[33] The Russian regime sees the ethnic Russians as natural supporters of Russian interests and subsidizes Russian ethnic political parties, politicians, and institutions in the Baltic States. At several times since the Baltic States gained independence, ethnic tensions stemming from the Russian minority have caused violent confrontations between the ethnic Russian minorities and the Estonian and Latvian governments. In the early-1990s, the tensions were increased due to the serious decline of the economy as the economies of the Baltic States made the adjustment to capitalist market economies. Since then, history has played a big role in ethnic tensions as the Baltic governments, representing the majority of public opinion, have taken down or moved communist-era memorials that, to Latvians and Estonians, represent some of the ugliest moments of their history. For the Russian ethnic minority, however, the memorials to the Red Army and its occupation of the Baltic States are a reminder of the glorious era of Soviet history. In 2007, the effort of the Estonian government to move a prominent memorial to the Red Army in Tallinn provoked a violent response from mobs of ethnic Russians. Both Tallinn and the heavily Russian northeast region saw violent demonstrations and violence that resulted in one death.[34]

This issue tends to be an important one for Latvia and Estonia, as they have large Russian ethnic minorities in their countries, and the status and role of minorities is an ongoing political issue in both those countries. In both Latvia and Estonia, the Russians who immigrated into those countries after the Soviet occupation of 1940 do not have the right to citizenship. Non-ethnic Estonians and Latvians have to go through a naturalization process, pass language exams, and prove long residence.[35] The noncitizen Russian ethnics remain in Estonia and Latvia but are given grey passports as officially "stateless" people. The Russian ethnics who remain in Estonia and Latvia have permission to live there and to vote in local elections, but as noncitizens, they cannot vote in national elections.[36]

In both Latvia and Estonia, there have been clashes and even some incidents of violence connected with the Russian minorities. Lithuania is in a different position—with only 6 percent of its population being ethnic Russian, along with small Ukrainian and Belarusian communities. In Lithuania's case, the ethnic minorities are smaller and more assimilated than in Estonia or Latvia. However, the intrepretation of history also plays a very important role in the Lithuanian relationship with Russia.[37]

Despite the history of ethnic minority tension in Estonia and Latvia, none of the Latvians and Estonians interviewed put the threat of internal security crises fueled by ethnic minorities high on their list of security concerns. Over time, this problem seems to be diminishing, with the aging of the large Russian workforce that was brought into Latvia and Estonia in the Soviet era and the ongoing assimilation of the workers' children, who, unlike their parents, are learning the national languages and are more integrated into the social and economic life of the individual country.[38]

To be sure, there are strong Russian nationalist groups and parties in both Latvia and Estonia, and they do receive financial support from Moscow. Theoretically, they could be used to provoke violent confrontation with the national governments or to demonstrate in favor of Russian interests. This was a real concern in the 1990s, and even as late as 2007, in Estonia, where some violent clashes centered around the Estonian government's action to remove a Soviet war memorial that was highly offensive to the majority of Estonians but seen as a symbol of Russian wartime glory by the Russian ethnic population.[39] In 1998, issues over war memorials to the Red

Army and Latvian government commemoration of the veterans of the Latvian Legion that had fought the Soviets alongside the Germans in World War II were part of a series of demonstrations and confrontations between the Latvian government and the Russian minority.[40] But as time goes on, the ethnic confrontations and level of dissatisfaction of the ethnic Russian communities of Latvia and Estonia have diminished, and ethnic relations are improving. In short, it is much harder today than in the past for Moscow to engineer a confrontation that would provide Russia an excuse to "protect" the ethnic Russian populations. Thus, while the minority issue is still a problem, none of the interviewees consider it one of the major Baltic concerns.

Economic Security.

The three Baltic States share some of the key long-term problems that Western Europe faces, namely, the long-term demographics of Europe that threaten national stability. Like the rest of Europe, the three Baltic States have aging populations and not enough babies born to maintain population levels. Most of those interviewed put the long-term economic stability of their countries as a serious concern.

Several of the interviewees commented on the problem of the "brain drain" that clearly exists for the Baltic countries. The three Baltic States are all exceptionally literate societies with excellent educational systems. As such, they produce yearly many highly qualified young people with excellent professional qualifications, as well as high fluency in English. Since they are EU states, there is nothing to inhibit talented young people from leaving their countries to find work elsewhere in Europe, and, in fact, bright younger people are using this opportunity. One Lithuanian noted that the better pay and economic conditions elsewhere in Europe have caused the loss of 300,000 Lithuanians who have emigrated for economic reasons since independence. Lithuania is the worst case within the Baltic countries for brain drain, but Latvia and, to a lesser extent, Estonia also have this problem. The Latvian and Lithuanian governments are addressing this and discussing government policies that will attract the young Latvians and Lithuanians back to their country. In the cases of the Baltic countries, the solution is to attract more investment and grow the economy again (after the hard times of the 2008-09 recession) to lure back the young workers they have lost.

However, in terms of economic security, the threat of Russian use of soft power against them was mentioned by several of those interviewed. One of the Estonian academics noted that Russia tries to use its soft power and investment to buy influence and to corrupt Baltic politicians, businesses, and institutions. A Latvian officer noted the problem in his country as well. An Estonian senior officer said that Russian investment and ownership of key infrastructure in his country is a security concern. That Russia would use its soft power to coerce neighboring states is not an unreasonable concern, given the influence that Moscow has gained over the Ukraine and Belarus by aggressive use of soft power. However, Russia has been reluctant to use blatant economic coercion against the Baltic States because such a strategy would likely backfire. The three Baltic States are all important transit routes for goods in and out of Russia, and many Russian enterprises would face economic disruption and higher prices if Russia used economic coercion against the Baltic States in too blatant a manner.[41]

Military Position of the Baltic States.

The Baltic States developed their armed forces very quickly and efficiently, receiving considerable aid and assistance from the Nordic nations and from NATO nations and the United States. The armed forces initially were built on conscription led by a professional cadre, but, in recent years, Latvia and Lithuania have gone over to a professional force, while Estonia retains conscription.[42] Beginning with the stated goal to join NATO announced in 1995, all three Baltic countries developed national security strategies on the Western model, and by 2005, they had developed fairly sophisticated national security strategies that included dealing with irregular as well as conventional threats. All the national security strategies of the Baltic States also address soft power and nonmilitary aspects of security, as well as purely military factors.[43]

Another key factor has been the willingness of all three Baltic States to build a credible national defense on their own. Prior to the economic crisis of 2008-09, they strove to build up their defense forces and infrastructure with the goal of meeting the 2 percent spending level of the GDP that NATO desires—but does not get—from its European members.[44] Since the economic crisis—in which all the Baltic nations drastically cut government expenditures, government employee pay, senior pensions, and military pay and expenditures—the spending on defense has been slow to increase to previous levels. However, the dose of hard medicine did work. After a very severe downturn, the three Baltic States sorted out their debt problem and now have a low rate of government borrowing. Estonia and Latvia have strong growth economies — in fact, they are at the top of the growing economies in the EU.[45] So the Baltic States are among the few nations to have come out of the economic crisis in good order and now have the capability to spend more on defense. Several of those interviewed said that since the Baltic economies are again on the rise, it is important to increase defense spending again. Several of those interviewed stated the opinion that Baltic defense spending was much too low, and no one argued for any further decreases in the national defense budget. One senior officer noted that, "It is embarrassing that my country spends so little on defense."[46]

The Baltic Consensus on Security.

The question of whether there is a unique view on security that is shared by the three Baltic States as a regional entity was posed to all 15 of the policymakers and shapers who were interviewed. The consensus was that there is no common view on security that is especially Baltic, but rather that the Baltic view on security is really more of a "New Europe" versus an "Old Europe" view. The concerns and perceptions of the threats to national security in the Baltic are, in the big picture, not fundamentally different than the positions common to the former Warsaw Pact states such as Poland, Hungary, and the Czech Republic, which joined NATO in the major expansion of NATO in 2004. In contrast to "Old Europe," the Eastern European NATO nations still see Russia as a serious problem that could become an overt threat, and therefore still view NATO's conventional military deterrence as very important. The Baltic States, along with the Eastern European NATO allies, see NATO as the *sine qua non* of their national security. Moreover, those interviewed all viewed U.S. security support and the U.S. presence in Europe as the central factors for their own security. Thus, it is not only NATO, but especially the U.S. relationship that was stressed by most of those interviewed, and this view was shared equally by the senior military officers and academics. Most of those interviewed stressed the U.S. presence in Europe, and the U.S. security guarantee of Europe remains the core of the Baltic States' own national security strategies. As one Latvian academic put it, "When you have the U.S. as your ally, then your national security is assured."[47] With NATO Article 5 guarantees in place in the NATO strategic concept, not even Russia would overtly challenge the independence of the three Baltic States.

In short, the U.S. military presence in Europe is very welcome in the Baltic States, and there is no desire to see it lessened or any fundamental changes enacted. A few of those interviewed noted that the discussions to increase Nordic and Baltic States' military cooperation were ongoing and welcome, but no one offered the view that these talks would produce any major results. As for their view on U.S. policy, those interviewed saw U.S. actions to remove some of the military forces from Europe and reorient toward the Pacific as perfectly understandable. As interviewees from all the Baltic States noted, the United States operates as a global power with global concerns and, as small states, they have to understand that. As one Estonian senior officer noted, "Militarily speaking Europe is pretty quiet while the US faces considerably more tension in Asia. So the US force redeployment makes perfect sense."[48]

Other Baltic policy makers also noted that, in terms of security, the Baltic States are "a fairly safe corner of Europe." The Baltic policymakers and shapers would prefer to see the U.S. presence in Europe remain strong, but none were especially alarmed by the reduction of U.S. forces—at least in the current political atmosphere. But all insisted that it is important that the Americans remain in Europe. As one Latvian senior officer noted, "The United States is the ONLY real security partner."[49] This view was echoed by all those interviewed. In short, there is no confidence that the EU or a NATO without the United States could be a true assurance of Baltic national security. All the interviewees believed the United States is the key partner. As one Lithuanian academic noted, "Who is going to choose Lithuania as an enemy if it has the United States as an ally?"[50]

All the interviewees acknowledged that maintaining the transatlantic alliance was a key factor in making policy in their nations. All the Baltic States sent troops to Iraq, and all are strongly committed with troops and civilian personnel to support the war in Afghanistan. As the interviewees pointed out, the Middle East and Afghanistan are scarcely of concern to the Baltic States; each Baltic nation took on the support of these conflicts with the main goal of cementing and supporting the transatlantic alliance. U.S. support is shown in other aspects of Baltic national policies. One Lithuanian academic stated:

> Lithuania voted with the US to deny Palestine a seat on the UNESCO [UN Educational, Scientific, and Cultural Organization] Council. Frankly, Lithuanians do not think much at all about the issue one way or another. But the vote was a way of showing support for the US.[51]

While stressing the importance of the U.S. relationship, several of the interviewees expressed the desire to see more cooperation with the EU on security matters. One Latvian member of parliament hoped that the EU would build more military cooperation in terms of creating multinational units for peacekeeping and stability operations. A Latvian senior official, lamenting that there was not really a joint Baltic States security policy, would like to see more cooperation between the states on military matters, such as more joint planning and more exercises and, most importantly, more Baltic nation joint bases and procurement. Yet, while several interviewees wanted to see an increase in the current level of security cooperation between the EU and the three Baltic States, no one favored such arrangements as a means of supplanting NATO or the transatlantic cooperation as the basis for their security. The general view in the Baltics is that the countries can and should do better in many respects concerning the support of European and multinational security relationships.

Particular National Views on Security.

In interviewing policymakers and shapers from all three nations, I found it easy to note national differences in the ways that people from each Baltic nation prioritized the security threats to their nation. For example, all the Lithuanians put energy security at the top of the national security challenges. This is because Lithuania is in the worst position of the three Baltic States in terms of energy dependence on Russia. Lithuania must import almost all its energy from outside. Since the shutdown of the Lithuanian nuclear plant, Lithuania is reliant on electricity from Belarus.

The nature of the electric grid in Lithuania is such that the main lines to the northern cities run through the Russian enclave of Kaliningrad. Lithuania depends almost completely on Russia for its supply of gas and oil and pays a high price. Currently, Lithuania is developing a natural gas port and better port facilities to ensure oil and gas imports. Latvia also depends highly upon Russia for energy, and the Latvians see this as a problem. Estonia is the one Baltic State that produces its own energy supplies (shale oil is mined in northeast Estonia) and does not depend on gas and oil pipelines from Russia.

Most of the Latvians interviewed put economic security at the top of their list of concerns. Latvia was badly hurt by the recent economic crisis and is recovering more slowly than Estonia. One Latvian also noted the purchase of a Latvian bank by a Russian consortium as causing security concerns in his country, as the Russian government could use Russian business interests to pressure Latvia. Lithuanians and Estonians also noted economic security as an important issue. However, the Baltic officials and academics interviewed did not see that overt Russian economic coercion was highly likely, because the consequences for Russia's provoking states important for the transit of its goods, and also EU member states, would likely hurt Russia even more than the Baltic States. Still, the Baltic States are looking to lessen vulnerabilities in the economic sector for, as one Estonian academic put it, "You can't count on the Russians always being rational."[52]

Lithuanians put the Russian information campaign high on the list of their national security threats. Latvians and Estonians also note the Russian campaign as a problem, but all gave it a lower priority. All the

Estonians noted that national cyber protection was an important security concern. This is understandable, because in April and May 2007, Estonia faced a large-scale, highly organized cyber attack that was designed to take down government websites and the websites and communications of the banks and large businesses. This coordinated attack was likely the work of Russian groups, although the Russian government denied any involvement.[53] Since that event, Estonia has been highly conscious of protecting its Internet system and has become a world leader in the study of cyber defense. From the Baltic viewpoint, this attack to disrupt the economy and society of Estonia was an example of the use of Russian "soft power" to coerce the Baltic States.

On the problems posed by internal minorities, some Latvians and Estonians mentioned the ethnic friction but basically noted that the ethnic problems, which were very serious in the 1990s, have receded in their countries and were fading with time. Although Russia asserts that one of its national security interests is to support and protect the rights of Russian ethnic people outside of Russia and could use the issue of Russian ethnic rights as a pretext to intervene, the Latvians and Estonians still put the internal security issues posed by Russian ethnics low on the list of security concerns. The Lithuanians have only a small Russian ethnic community today (6 percent), and the Russians in Lithuania are fairly well assimilated. Unlike in Estonia and Latvia, there are no Russian major ethnic political parties.

The Baltic View of U.S. Policy and the Importance of Credibility.

None of the policymakers and shapers I interviewed thought that the question of where the Baltic States might diverge from U.S. policy and views was especially relevant. Most commented that since the Baltic States are so small, any comment or critique they have toward the United States would not likely have any effect on the big picture of U.S. policy. If the same question had been posed to a British, French, or German policymaker or shaper, I would have received a long and detailed critique of U.S. policy and world view in particular, with a critique on U.S. policy in Iraq and Afghanistan, and in dealing with international terrorism. In contrast, the Baltics are sparing in their criticism of U.S. policy — unless it would directly impact their region. This comes from the perspective that they ought to save their critique and comments on U.S. policy for the moment when it really matters.

One Latvian academic noted that the United States has declined in power due to the ongoing war on terror, the conflict in Iraq, and the weak state of the U.S. economy in the last 4 years. Estonians and Latvians noted that there are concerns in the Baltic States about the relative decline of U.S. power and, as one put it, there are "unvocalized concerns that the U.S. might not stay in Europe" (meaning, a military presence). However, whatever concerns the Baltic States have about U.S. policies, they cannot do much about them. As a Latvian academic noted, "Latvia is in no position to disagree, so we'll just have to adjust to the US."[54] An Estonian academic noted that the Baltic approach, "is to avoid confrontation. The three Baltic States will do everything they can to maintain NATO and the transatlantic link."[55] Half of the respondents, representing all three Baltic countries, said that maintaining their international credibility is of utmost importance. Therefore, when they do have something important to say, the United States might be more ready to listen.

The Baltic policymakers and shapers are very aware of the need to maintain their credibility in the eyes of NATO, the EU, and especially the United States. One Latvian academic commented that:

> We don't want to be seen as just three countries that have unfriendly relations with Russia. The three Baltic States have been rebranded as NATO nations and the Baltic countries want to be seen as countries that can deal with the new style of threats to NATO such as cyber and energy. This is why the Estonians have established the NATO Cyber Center of Excellence in Tallinn and the Lithuanians have set up the NATO Center for Energy Policy in Vilnius.[56]

Clearly, the Baltic States want to be seen as making a useful contribution to the alliance and getting visibility in NATO and the EU on issues of broad concern. Within the EU, the three Baltic States want to be seen as modern, competent, and cooperative, which is why the three states try to avoid direct confrontation with Russia.[57]

In fact, the people interviewed were all far more critical of their own national governments than of U.S. policies. One Latvian senior official noted that, "Latvia sees threats but is not allocating the resources to deal with them."[58] A Latvian member of Parliament noted that his country should do more to support the UN and international operations. He also noted that the three Baltic States could do more in terms of partnership. In the interviews, a common critique of national policy was that their countries could and should do more for their own security, and that Europe should do more as well.

The Baltics and the U.S.-Russian Reset.

Several of those interviewed mentioned the U.S.-Russia "reset," which had been put into place by the Obama administration in 2009. The consensus from Baltic policymakers and shapers was that the Russia reset has been a failure. Russian policy and behavior, or even the tone and style of Russia's statements about NATO and the West, have not substantially changed since 2009. Russia has not cooperated in a meaningful or friendly way with the West. Russia's military doctrine of 2010 lists NATO as its top enemy. Russia continues to support Assad's Syrian regime; Russia continues to block serious sanctions on Iran, and it also provides Iran with weapons and nuclear technology. In 2012, Russia even expelled the U.S. Agency for International Development from Russia after 2 decades of that agency's presence. In the case of Russia's relationship with the Baltic countries, no substantial improvements have been noted. There are no serious crises, and trade goes on as before, but there has been no thaw in the ice in the Baltic region. Since the people I interviewed all have extensive knowledge of Russia and Russian affairs, the failure of the Russian reset came as no surprise, and no government in the Baltic region, while officially welcoming the reset initiative, had any expectations that things would change.

However, one Estonian academic did note that, ironically, the U.S.-Russia reset had inadvertently worked in favor of the Baltic States' security. He noted that because the United States felt the need to reassure the Baltics and the Eastern Europeans on the reset policy, NATO moved forward on developing contingency defense plans for the region—an item that had been put on hold before the reset. The U.S. and NATO reassurance measures included endorsing the NATO air police mission in the Baltics until 2018, greater U.S. and NATO national presence in military exercises in the region, and the deployment of Patriot missiles to Poland. In return for the reset, the Baltics gained additional U.S. and NATO presence in the form of actual troops and U.S. military presence, which the Estonian official noted was far more important and far more useful in building Baltic security than any symbolic statements.

CONCLUSION

The Baltic policymakers and shapers interviewed for this monograph do not foresee any major changes in the security situation in the Baltic States in the near future. They do not see any major change in their relations with the United States and NATO in the future. Indeed, none of the policymakers and shapers wanted to see any major changes in the U.S. and Baltic States' security relationship. All see the United States as an indispensable ally and want it to maintain a strong leadership role in NATO and a capable American military presence in Europe.

Interviews with Baltic experts and leaders indicate a strong consensus on the key issues of security. While there are clear differences in how people from each Baltic State would prioritize the threats in terms of their own nation, all agreed that the biggest security problem for the Baltic is Russia and its policies. No one pointed to any immediate danger or listed a direct military confrontation as the major security threat in the future. The Baltic States feel militarily secure as long as NATO and the United States maintain the policy of collective defense. Essentially, the Baltics are well aware that Russia might use soft power against them and plan accordingly.

The Baltic leaders have an understanding of Russia that is soundly borne out by the facts and their ongoing close relations with Russia. Their view of the U.S.-Russia reset is soundly grounded. While the Baltic leaders distrust the Russians, they are also careful not to overplay the theme in dealing with Western European nations so as to maintain their credibility. Maintaining their national credibility inside NATO and the EU as reliable diplomatic, economic, and military partners is key to understanding the Baltic national positions on security policy. Whatever their private views on the wisdom of the U.S. involvement in Iraq or Afghanistan, or the NATO mission in Kosovo, the three Baltic States will remain strong partners and contributors of troops, funds, and expertise to U.S. and NATO actions. The Baltic countries, although limited in resources, will also continue to be strong supporters of NATO and Western policies.

RECOMMENDATIONS FOR U.S. LANDPOWER

The three Baltic nations remain strong U.S. and NATO allies currently and for the future, committed to supporting the NATO alliance and NATO operations. The strong commitment of the three Baltic States to send forces, without caveats, to Iraq and Afghanistan show the seriousness of intent in the three Baltic States.

The three Baltic States perceive that Russia is a security problem, although not an immediate military threat. Still, for the long term, the Baltic States support a policy based on deterrence and capable homeland defense. The Baltic perspective is based on a very deep understanding of Russia and is grounded in a realistic assessment of recent Russian behavior toward the Baltic and Eastern European states. U.S. strategists should not ignore this perspective.

There is a sense of unease noted in the interviews with the Baltic policymakers and shapers that the United States has gone far enough in cutting its military forces based in Europe—perhaps even too far. In the eyes of the Baltic States' leaders, nothing can replace the actual presence of U.S. forces on the ground and the visible commitment of U.S. forces. First, the United States ought to seriously rethink the idea to cut U.S. forces in the European Command (EUCOM) back to only two brigades. But if the cuts happen, then that should be the final line, as too small of a U.S. force in Europe would likely cause serious problems of confidence within NATO. Elites in the three Baltic States see the problem as a lack of visible capability of European NATO nations and of the United States, as well as the military capabilities of their own countries.

The United States, and particularly the U.S. Army, can do several things to improve the level of defense cooperation at a low cost. The Baltic States have created NATO centers of excellence in cyber (Estonia) and energy security (Lithuania). Both areas are of great interest to U.S. military educational institutions. The U.S. Army War College, the U.S. Army Command and General Staff College, and perhaps the National Defense University should become more closely engaged with both these centers and consider a formal close exchange of academic personnel. The U.S. military schools can engage with the Cyber Center and the Center on Energy Security, which are both cutting-edge institutions in terms of developing research and course curricula, to the advantage of the U.S. institutions.

The United States needs to participate in and support further military contingency planning for the Eastern European region, including defense scenarios in the Baltic area. The contingency planning needs to be backed up with an increased level of military exercises with the Baltic States and Eastern European NATO allies. If the United States continues to cut forces in EUCOM, then it needs to visibly compensate by detailing land, air, and naval forces currently based in the United States to engage in large training exercises in Eastern Europe. Flying in one or two U.S. brigades to participate in maneuvers in Poland might be considered.

The deployment of U.S. anti-aircraft and missile defense units to Eastern Europe would be welcomed by the Eastern Europeans and the Baltic States. Again, any visible U.S. presence, in the form of exercises, port calls, air police units, and so on, is seen as a true symbol of U.S. commitment. If possible, this ought to be increased. Again, the costs envisioned are relatively modest.

Finally, the three Baltic States are all concerned with national territorial defense, and all have reserve forces. The Estonians, in particular, have a plan to build up their reserves by 2018. The programs to train, develop, equip, and support the Baltic States reserve forces should be given additional support from the United States and an assessment should be made as to how the United States might support the equipment needs of the Baltic Reserve forces so that they are fully interoperable with NATO forces. A modest increase in support of the National Guard partnerships with each Baltic State (Estonia is partnered with Maryland, Lithuania with Pennsylvania, and Latvia with Michigan) would provide reassurance in the eyes of the Baltic States at a modest cost.

ENDNOTES

1. For an overview of the Russian 2000 and 2003 *Defense Policy Papers*, which outline Russia's hostility to NATO, see Marcel de Haas, "Putin's Security Policy in the Past, Present and Future," *Baltic Defence Review*, Vol. 2, No. 12, 2004, pp. 39-59. Russia was concerned about NATO enlargement when it happened and still sees the expansion of NATO as a major threat. For an analysis of the latest official Russian military doctrine approved by President Medvedev, which sees NATO as a "military danger," see Keir Giles, "The Military Doctrine of the Russian Federation 2010," *NATO Research Review*, NATO Defense College, February 2010.

2. See Algirdas Degatis, "The Transatlantic Rift: Ideological Roots and Implications for Central and Eastern Europe," *Lithuanian Annual Strateguc Review 2005*, Vilnius, Lithuania: Strategic Research Center, 2006, pp. 9-52.

3. For an excellent history of the development of the three Baltic States with commentary on recent events, see Andres Kasekamp, *A History of the Baltic States*, London, UK: Palgrave, 2010.

4. A complete review of Baltic States' defense spending is found in Dr. Eric J. De Bakker and Dr. Robert Beeres, "A Comparative Financial Analysis of Military Expenditures on the Baltic States, 2000-2010," *Baltic Security and Defence Review*, Vol. 14, Issue 1, 2012, pp. 5-23.

5. The breakdown of the interviews is as follows: Lithuania: Two senior military officers, three academics; Latvia: One member of Parliament, one senior government official, one senior military officer, two academics; Estonia: One senior military

officer, four academics. I knew all of the interviewees before the interviews, and I have known 10 of them for more than 3 years.

6. Personal Interview with a senior Latvian official.

7. See Kasekamp, pp. 99-105.

8. *Ibid.*, pp. 128-131.

9. For details on the Soviet repression in Estonia in 1941-45, see the Estonian International Commission for the Investigation of Crimes Against Humanity, *Estonia 1940-1945*, Tallinn, Estonia: Estonian Foundation for the Investigation of Crimes Against Humanity, 2005.

10. Kasekamp, pp. 141-146.

11. In one wave of deportations in 3 days in March, 43,000 Latvians, including women and children, were rounded up and deported to Siberia, where many perished. In just this one wave of deportations, 92,000 Baltic people were sent to Siberia. In all, hundreds of thousands of people from these small states were sent to the gulags and to settlements in Siberia and Central Asia. See Paul Rothenhäusler and Hans-Ueli Sonderegger, eds., *Errinerung an den Roten Holocaust* (*Remembering the Roten Holocaust*), Stäfe Switzerland: Rothenhäusler Verlag, 1999, pp. 58-69.

12. For a detailed analysis of the largest and most effective resistance movement in the Baltics, see Vylius Leskys, "'Forest Brothers' 1945: The Culmination of the Lithuanian Partisan Movement," *Baltic Security and Defence Review*, Vol. 11, No. 1, 2009.

13. For the whole story of the history commission that revised the Soviet history of the 1939 Pact, see Heike Lindpere, *Molotov-Ribbentrop Pact: Challenging Soviet History*, Tallinn, Estonia: Estonian Foreign Policy Institute, 2009. On the Soviet denunciation of the treaty's legality, see *Ibid.*, pp. 173-195.

14. Kasekamp, p. 196.

15. *Ibid.*, p. 197.

16. My office is located 100 meters from a large grey building that was the Regional Headquarters of the NKVD/KGB for southern Estonia. The holding and torture cells of the KGB in the basement are now preserved as a museum. Indeed, it is easy to find many former prisoners of the Soviet gulags in Tartu, Estonia. The Tartu KGB Museum contains many documents, artifacts, and photos of the Soviet gulags, some items donated by still living local people. I have met a number of Estonians who spent time in the gulags. I have also met a number of Estonians my age who were born in Kazakhstan and similar places — something not at all unusual in the Baltic States.

17. Russian opinion polls show the success of Putin's information campaign against the Baltic States and NATO among the Russian population. Latvia and Lithuania are seen as two of the three nations most hostile to Russia, and Russian opinion polls in 2007 showed that 42 percent of Russians saw Lithuania as "very hostile" to Russia. See Leonid Karabeshkin, "Russian-Lithuanian Relations: Between Negative Perception Stereotypes and Pragmatic Cooperation," *Lithuanian Annual Strategic Review 2006*, Vilnius, Lithuania: Strategic Research Center, 2007, pp. 65-83, especially p. 82.

18. On Baltic States' economic reforms in the 1990s, see Kasekamp, pp. 181-183.

19. See Zaneta Ozolina, "Crisis Prevention or Intervention: Latvia's Response to the Proposed Russian Security Guarantees," Eric Stern and Dan Hansen, eds., *Crisis Management in a Transitional Society: The Latvian Experience*, Stockholm, Sweden: Försvarshögskolan, 2000, pp. 188-215.

20. Kasekamp, pp. 183-185.

21. Linas Linkevicius, "Participation of the Lithuanian Troops in International Peace Support Operations," *Baltic Defence Review,* Vol. 1, Issue No. 1, 1999.

22. Brigadier General Michael Clemmeson, "NATO Interoperability and the Baltic Defence College," *Baltic Defence Review,* Vol. 1 Issue No. 1, 1999.

23. One Latvian senior official interviewed spelled out several procurement and equipment issues that he would like to see conducted on a three-country basis instead of the current national basis. A Latvian member of parliament interviewed said he would like to see more than three-nation military units, such as the Baltic Battalion of the 1990s, that would be available to support EU and NATO peace operations as a contingency force. While all three Baltic nations cooperate very well on military training and conduct joint exercises, the one barrier to wider cooperation among the states is deciding what equipment to procure and how to allocate the contracts among the Baltic States.

24. Personal Interview with a senior Estonian official.

25. The Baltic Defence College was part of this lobbying effort by hosting a workshop on the new NATO strategic concept that featured leading Baltic politicians and academics. The proceedings of the workshop revealed the need to maintain collective security as the key NATO strategy. See *Proceedings of a Workshop on NATO's Strategic Concept*, October 15-16, 2009, Tartu, Estonia, published in the *Baltic Security and Defence Review*, Vol. 12, Issue 1, 2010.

26. See *The Military Doctrine of the Russian Federation*, approved by Russian Federation Presidential Edict on February 5, 2010. Translation by the SRAS-School of Russian and Asian Studies. The main external threats to the Russian Federation are as follows: The main external military dangers are: a. the desire to endow the force potential of the North Atlantic Treaty Organization (NATO) with global functions carried out in violation of the norms of international law and to move the military infrastructure of NATO member countries closer to the borders of the Russian Federation, including by expanding the bloc; b. the attempts to destabilize the situation in individual states and regions and to undermine strategic stability; c. the deployment and buildup of troop contingents from foreign states and groups of states on the territories of states contiguous with the Russian Federation and its allies and also in adjacent waters. . . .

27. In a 2008 speech, Russian President Dmitri Medvedev has openly stated that Russian policy is to build a sphere of influence in the nations around its borders. See Andrew Kramer, "Russia

Claims its Sphere of Influence in the World," *The New York Times*, September 1, 2008.

28. See *Active Engagement, Modern Defence. Strategic Concept for the Defence and Security of the Members of the North Atlantic Treaty Organization*. Adopted by the Heads of State and Government at the NATO Summit in Lisbon, November 19-20, 2010, available from *www.nato.int/strategic-concept/pdf/Strat_Concept_web_en.pdf*.

29. Airis Rikveilis, "Strategic Culture in Latvia: Seeking, Defining, and Developing," *Baltic Security and Defence Review*, Vol. 9, 2007, pp. 196-197.

30. See Andres Mäe, "Vulnerability of Interdependent Energy Relations: Energy Strategies of Small Countries," *Estonian Foreign Policy Yearbook 2010*, Tallinn, Estonia: Estonian Foreign Policy Institute, 2011, pp. 123-169.

31. For an analysis of Russia's media campaign against small neighbors, see Nerijus Maliukevicius, "Russia's Information Policy in Lithuania: The Spread of Soft Power of Information Geopolitics?" *Baltic Security and Defence Review*, Vol. 9, 2007, pp. 150-170.

32. On Russia's approach to soft power and information, see Robert Ortturg, "Russia's Use of PR as a Foreign Policy Tool," *Russian Analytical Digest*, Vol. 81, June 2010, pp. 7-10. See also "Russian World-Russia's Soft Power Approach to Compatriot's Policy," *Russian Analytical Digest*, Vol. 81, June 2010, pp. 2-4.

33. See the *CIA World Factbook* for recent statistics on the ethnic makeup of the Baltic States. In Latvia, the population is 59.3 percent ethnic Latvian, 27.8 percent Russian, 3.6 percent Belarusian, and 2.5 percent Ukrainian. Of the Latvians, 37.5 percent are Russian speakers. In Estonia, 68.7 percent of the population is ethnic Estonian, and 25.6 percent are Russian or Russian speakers.

34. Heiko Pääbo, "War of Memories: Explaining the 'Memorials War' in Estonia," *Baltic Security and Defence Review*, Vol. 10, 2008, pp. 5-28.

35. On the ethnicity and citizenship issues in the Baltic States per the Russian minority, see Kasekamp, pp. 184-187.

36. On the citizenship issue and ethnic friction, see Andris Runcis, "The Citizenship Issue as a Creeping Crisis," *Crisis Management in a Transitional Society: The Latvian Experience*, Stockholm, Sweden: Försvarshögskolan, 2000, pp. 61-97.

37. Česlovas Laurinavičius, "The Role of History in the Relationship between Lithuania and Russia," *Lithuanian Annual Strateguc Review 2005*, Vilnius, Lithuania: Strategic Research Center, 2006, pp. 109-125.

38. As a teacher at Tartu University, I can add some of my own experience to this. Every year I teach a graduate class of 45 students who are mostly Estonian and include ethnic Russians as well as ethnic Estonians. The ethnic Russians can speak Estonian, although their English tends to be more fluent than their Estonian, and they also tend to be employed by Estonian firms. That the ethnic Russians are able to meet the very high entrance standards of Tartu University shows that the Estonian education system has not failed the ethnic Russian population. The ethnic Russians are fully included in university life. Some of my ethnic Russian students have told me of visiting their relatives in Russia, but they seem to have little interest in becoming Russians or holding a deep attachment to the Russian state. The ethnic Estonian relationship to Russia seems to be more of a connection with their cousins back in the old country. Sometimes my ethnic Russian students note that they have been brought up to speak a more educated form of Russian, such as that spoken in Moscow, while their relatives in Russia sometimes use local dialects that are hard for them to understand.

39. See Pääbo.

40. Daina Bleiere and Aivars Stranga, "The Latvian Russian Crisis of 1997," Eric Stern and Dan Hansen, eds., *Crisis Management in a Transitional Society: The Latvian Experience*, Stockholm, Sweden: Försvarshögskolan, 2000, pp. 216-259.

41. Ozolina, "Crisis Prevention or Intervention: Latvia's Response to the Proposed Russian Security Guarantees," pp. 192-193.

42. Grazina Miniotairte, "The Construction of the Model of the Army in Lithuaniaś Politcal Discourse," *Lithuanian Annual Strategic Review 2008*, Vilnius, Lithuania: Strategic Research Center, 2008, pp. 183-202.

43. On Baltic States security strategies, see Vaidotas Urbelis, "Lithuanian Deterrence Strategy," *Lithuanian Annual Strategic Review 2005*, Vilnius, Lithuania: Strategic Research Center, 2005, pp 169-193. See also Kristine Doronenkova, "Latvia's Security Perspective: An Analysis of Official Sources," Zaneta Ozolina, ed., *Rethinking Security*, Zinätne, Latvian Search Engine, 2010, pp. 306-324; Vaidotas Urbelis, "Lithuania's Strategic Culture," in *Lithuanian Annual Strategic Review 2006*, Vilnius, Lithuania: Strategic Research Center, 2007, pp. 193-207. See also Rikveilis, pp. 187-209.

44. For a detailed overview of Baltic State military budgets and military infrastructure building, see Bakker and Beeres.

45. The three Baltic States had exceptional economic growth before the 2008-09 downturn: The Lithuanian GDP grew at 8 percent per annum before 2008. Latvian GDP grew at a rate of 10 percent in 2006-07. The Estonian GDP grew at a rate of 8 percent from 2003-07. In 2009, the Lithuanian GDP dropped 15 percent; the Latvian GDP dropped 18 percent; and the Estonian GDP dropped 14.3 percent. Since then, all the countries have seen significant economic recovery, with Lithuanian GDP growing 1.3 percent in 2010 and 5.8 percent in 2011. The Latvian economy has been growing since 2010, and since 2010 Estonia has had the highest economic growth rate in the EU. See *CIA World Factbook* for statistics.

46. Personal interview with a senior official.

47. Personal interview with a Latvian academic.

48. Personal interview with a senior Estonian officer.

49. Personal interview with a senior Latvian officer.

50. Lithuanian academic noted.

51. Personal interview with a Lithuanian academic.

52. Personal interview with an Estonian academic.

53. For more on the the cyber attacks on Estonia, see Robert Ashmore, "Impact of Alleged Russian Cyber Attacks," *Baltic Security and Defence Review*, Vol. 11, 2010, pp. 4-39.

54. Personal interview with a Latvian academic.

55. Personal interview with an Estonian academic.

56. Personal interview with a Latvian academic.

57. Gediminas Vitkus and Jurate Novagrockiene, "The Impact of Lithuania on EU Council Decision-Making," *Lithuanian Annual Strategic Review 2007*, Vilnius, Lithuania: Strategic Research Center, 2007, pp. 91-123.

58. Personal interview with a senior Latvian official.

www.ingramcontent.com/pod-product-compliance
Lightning Source LLC
Chambersburg PA
CBHW080613290526
45790CB00007B/2755